Original title:
Clouded Contradictions

Copyright © 2024 Creative Arts Management OÜ
All rights reserved.

Author: Nathaniel Blackwood
ISBN HARDBACK: 978-9916-90-590-6
ISBN PAPERBACK: 978-9916-90-591-3

Twisted Skies

Clouds swirl in shades of grey,
Whispers of storms that drift and play.
The sun hides behind a veil of dread,
As shadows dance where angels tread.

Lightning flashes, a sudden spark,
Illuminating the cold and dark.
Winds howl like forgotten cries,
Beneath the weight of twisted skies.

Stars catch breath in silent night,
Caught in the web of fading light.
Planets spin with a haunting grace,
While twilight drapes its mystic lace.

Hope flickers, a fragile flame,
In the chaos, we feel the blame.
Yet within the tempest, strength lies,
We stand resilient under twisted skies.

Indecision's Serenade

A fork in the road, a heart in doubt,
Whispers of choice, a restless route.
Left or right? The path is unclear,
Each step forward brings waves of fear.

The clock ticks on, moments slip past,
Each second weighs heavy, shadows cast.
Dreams collide, realities blur,
Caught in the grip of thoughts that stir.

Voices echo in silent halls,
Options fade like old, cracked walls.
What if's linger, a haunting tune,
While stars watch and the night grows soon.

Yet amidst the haze, a light will glow,
To guide the heart where it longs to go.
Indecision sings a bittersweet song,
But within the struggle, we all belong.

The Pull of the Unfathomable

Tides of fate pull at my soul,
Whispers of dreams that make me whole.
Distant echoes from the deep,
Secrets buried that long to seep.

Stars align in a cosmic dance,
Every heartbeat a fleeting chance.
The unknown calls, a lover's claim,
In shadows deep, I hear its name.

Waves crash against the shores of time,
Each crest a rhythm, a silent rhyme.
The vast expanse pulls at my core,
A mystery that I must explore.

With every breath, I feel the lure,
Of something greater, vast, and pure.
In the depths where fears are laid,
I find my strength in the unfathomable shade.

Between Dreams and Reality

In the twilight where visions blend,
A world unseen, where shadows bend.
Fragments of thought dance and glide,
Between the known and dreams inside.

A whisper breezes through the night,
Inviting hearts to take flight.
Illusions shimmer, fade in gold,
A tapestry of stories told.

Reality flickers like candlelight,
Doubts loom large, yet dreams feel right.
The line grows thin, a fragile seam,
Where hope entwines with every dream.

In this space, we learn to soar,
Finding magic behind closed doors.
Between dreams and what seems so real,
Lies a truth that we all can feel.

The Delicate Dance

In twilight's glow, they twist and sway,
With whispered steps, they find their way.
The music swells, a soft romance,
Two souls entwined in a delicate dance.

Around them, shadows flicker and fade,
Each fleeting moment, a memory made.
With hearts in sync, they take a chance,
Lost in the rhythm of their sweet dance.

Through the silence, their laughter rings,
As stars above start spreading their wings.
In every glance, a fleeting glance,
They breathe the magic of their dance.

As dawn approaches, they hold tight,
A fleeting spark in the morning light.
Though time may steal their sweet romance,
They'll hold forever their delicate dance.

Beneath Layers of Vapors

Misty mornings, shrouded in gray,
Whispers of dreams begin to sway.
Beneath layers, secrets reside,
In the quiet, the whispers confide.

Softly they swirl, like thoughts unspoken,
In the silence, no hearts are broken.
Ancient stories fade in the haze,
Lost in the fog of forgotten days.

Each breath of air, a tale unfolds,
Wrapped in silver, the world withholds.
Embers of light dance in the mist,
In the shadows, there lies a twist.

With every step, the vapors shift,
Guiding the heart, a gentle lift.
Beneath layers of vapors, we seek,
The whispers of truth, both tender and bleak.

Stirrings of Unrest

Whispers creep through shadowed lanes,
Footsteps echo, breaking chains.
Hearts aflame with rising fire,
Longing for a world inspired.

Voices rise, a swelling tide,
Nations rally, side by side.
Fingers pointing, fists held high,
Underneath the stormy sky.

Change is brewing in the night,
Dreams ignited, burning bright.
Courage found in every soul,
As we march towards our goal.

The Tension of Silence

In the stillness, shadows play,
Words unspoken drift away.
Heavy hearts, the air feels thick,
Each glance shared, a secret flick.

A moment's pause, breath caught tight,
Lost in thoughts, the fading light.
Echoes linger of what's lost,
In this silence, we bear the cost.

What's left unsaid hangs like smoke,
Promises made, yet never broke.
Tension crackles in the dark,
Waiting for a whispered spark.

In Between the Lines

Pages turn, stories unfold,
Truths are glimpsed, and secrets told.
Words may dance, but silence speaks,
Hidden meanings, the heart seeks.

In the margins, thoughts reside,
Between the words, where dreams hide.
Readers lost in distant space,
Finding solace in the trace.

Every chapter, every plot,
In the layers, wisdom's caught.
Dive deeper, seek the rhymes,
Life's reflections in borrowed times.

Shadows of the Past

Echoes of a time now gone,
Memories linger, dusk till dawn.
Faded photographs, tales of yore,
Whispering secrets, forevermore.

Footsteps tread on ancient ground,
In their silence, lost are found.
Ghosts that dance in twilight's glow,
Bearing stories we can't know.

History carved in silent stone,
Lessons learned, yet oft alone.
From the shadows, lessons cast,
In the light, we hold the past.

Chasing Fleeting Comfort

In the hush of twilight's grace,
We seek a warm embrace.
With shadows close behind,
We weave through thoughts confined.

Yet whispers of the past,
In memories that last.
They dance like autumn leaves,
Fleeting comfort, our heart grieves.

We chase the softest glow,
A fire that ebbs low.
Each sigh a sweet surrender,
We fall, we rise, we wander.

In silence, we align,
With dreams we dare define.
But comfort, like a dream,
Slips through the seams, it seems.

Illusions of the Ether

In the stillness of the night,
Stars flicker with delight.
They whisper secrets old,
In cosmic tales retold.

Like shadows dancing light,
Illusions take their flight.
What's real and what's a game,
Beyond the stars, no shame.

In the vastness, we exist,
Chasing what we've missed.
Threads of dreams entwined,
In the ether, we find.

Yet truth eludes our grasp,
In the silence, we gasp.
To touch the unseen thread,
In illusion, we tread.

The Fork in the Path

Two roads diverge in the wood,
Each beckons where it could.
One lined with stones so clear,
The other cloaked in fear.

With every choice we make,
A new dawn starts to break.
But hesitate we do,
In the shadows, doubt grew.

The maps we draw in sand,
Fleeting, like a hand.
Yet the heart knows the way,
Through night and into day.

At the fork, we must stand,
With the fate close at hand.
And trust in the unknown,
A journey not alone.

Ephemeral Questions

In the quiet of the mind,
Questions linger, unkind.
What is time but a breath?
A riddle wrapped in death?

We ponder in the night,
Chasing shadows of light.
Each thought, a fleeting spark,
In the depths, it grows dark.

Why do we seek the truth,
When lies lie in our youth?
Ephemeral, they gleam,
Fleeting as a dream.

So we ask, but never know,
What lies beyond the flow?
In questions, we are lost,
To find ourselves, the cost.

Cascading Paradoxes

In the silence loud, they call,
Shadows dance, yet do not fall.
Truths collide in twisted ways,
Lost in thoughts that clutch and graze.

Rivers run with whispered lies,
Underneath the vastened skies.
Time unwinds in gentle sweeps,
Secrets buried, buried deep.

Mirrors break but still reflect,
Faced with choices we reject.
Light and dark, a tangled thread,
Chasing dreams that swirl like dread.

Echoes echo in the night,
Flickering like firelight.
Cascades shift, and all seems still,
In the whirl, we seek the thrill.

The Hearts' Crossroads

Two paths merge where shadows meet,
In the silence, heartbeats greet.
Forking roads both dark and bright,
Choices echo in the night.

Whispers linger, soft and slow,
Where to tread? We do not know.
Hope rises like a gentle flame,
But fear clings like a heavy name.

In the stillness, visions clear,
Every step, a hidden fear.
What if love would lead us right?
What if dreams fade with the light?

At each crossroad, stars align,
Fate will guide with subtle sign.
In the journey, we will find,
The heart's truth that's intertwined.

Ephemeral Whispers

Softly spoken, fleeting sounds,
Life's a dance on fragile grounds.
Moments fade like morning dew,
Each a brush of something new.

Echoes linger, then they're gone,
Chasing light at each new dawn.
Fleeting shadows, swift and sly,
Life's a whisper, quick to fly.

In the twilight, secrets sigh,
As the stars light up the sky.
Beauty lingers in the air,
Only felt, no need for dare.

Hold the now, but gently loose,
In the dance, we find our muse.
Life's a thread that weaves away,
In whispers, night merges with day.

Refracted Thoughts

Shards of light in prism's sway,
Color dances, shapes convey.
Twisted angles, thoughts collide,
In the spectrum, we confide.

Filters live in palettes wide,
Where reflections softly hide.
Thoughts refract in playful glee,
Fragments whisper, set them free.

Through the lens, the world expands,
Logic crumbles, breaks like sand.
Vision blurs, yet shines so bright,
In confusion, there's delight.

Dancing echoes, hues entwined,
In the chaos, truth defined.
Refracted thoughts won't stay still,
In the chaos, dreams fulfill.

Mists of the Heart

In silence, whispers weave like fog,
Dreams entwined within the haze.
Lost in thoughts, I seek a guide,
In the shadows, my heart lays.

Beneath the surface, secrets stir,
Veiled passions slowly rise.
In every breath, a soft allure,
Through the mists, our truth lies.

With every sigh, the air grows thick,
Emotions dance like fleeting light.
In tender moments, hearts can tick,
Until the dawn reveals the night.

So let us wander, hand in hand,
Through swirling dreams that softly part.
In this embrace, we'll understand,
The beauty found in the mists of heart.

The Dichotomy Dance

In shadows deep, two figures glide,
Each with grace, yet worlds apart.
One seeks the light, one seeks to hide,
In this dance, they play their part.

Fates entwined in twirling steps,
A balance held on fragile ground.
Both are lost, and yet, adept,
In the silence, a truth is found.

Within the clash, a spark ignites,
A melody so bittersweet.
In every bend, in all the heights,
The dichotomy feels complete.

Embrace the rhythm, lose control,
Let your heart set forth to prance.
In shadows' depth, we find our soul,
In this eternal dichotomy dance.

Shattered Illusions

Reflections crack, a fractured dream,
What once was whole is now a shard.
Through glassy eyes, we try to glean,
The truths that lie beneath the guard.

In every fragment, stories lie,
Of hopes and fears, both intertwined.
With tender care, we touch the sky,
Yet stumble, lost, as if blind.

From shadows cast by memories bright,
We gather pieces of the past.
With every step, we chase the light,
But some illusions fade too fast.

So gather strength from what remains,
Though pains may linger, love persists.
In shattered parts, our spirit gains,
The beauty found in broken lists.

Between the Sun and the Storm

A tender glow, the sun will rise,
While thunder rumbles in the deep.
In this space where contrast lies,
A battle rages while we sleep.

Clouds collide, a dance of fate,
The light and dark, a woven thread.
With every breath, we contemplate,
The moments shared, the words unsaid.

In gentle rays, a hope ignites,
Yet harsh winds blow, there's tension still.
Between the sun and stormy nights,
We seek a balance, find our will.

So let us navigate this space,
Where shadows play and daylight warms.
In this embrace, we find our place,
Between the sun and the gathering storms.

The Mirage of Certainty

In the desert of doubt we roam,
Searching for truths we call home.
Mirages shimmer, rise and fall,
What we hold dear, could it be all?

Waves of answers crash and break,
Every choice we make, a stake.
Certainty dances on shifting sands,
Guided only by fleeting hands.

We chase the sun, yet it eludes,
Wrapped in a cloak of changing moods.
Promises whisper like sand in wind,
In this quest for sure, where to begin?

A moment of clarity, then it fades,
Where light is cast, a shadow wades.
In the mirage's truth, we must trust,
For in uncertainty, there's also rust.

A Paradoxical Palette

Brushstrokes clash in vibrant dance,
Colors warping, lost in chance.
What is chaos, what is grace?
A paradox in every space.

Reds of passion, blues of woe,
Each hue telling tales we know.
Layering love with shades of fear,
Beauty formed from what's unclear.

In shadows cast by brightening light,
We find our dreams in the night.
Gray whispers blend with hues so bold,
The palette shifts, the story told.

Each canvas breathes a different voice,
In contradictions, we rejoice.
From discord, harmony will rise,
A paradox lies in every guise.

Dusk and Dawn

At dusk, the day begins to sigh,
Painted skies, a farewell cry.
Golden rays, a fleeting glow,
As night unveils its silken show.

Stars emerge from veiled haze,
Whispers of night, a softened blaze.
In shadows deep, the world transforms,
In quietude, the heart warms.

Dawn approaches, with gentle grace,
Fingers of light in a warm embrace.
Daybreak's kiss, the softest hue,
Promises born anew, so true.

In the cycle of end and start,
Dusk and dawn, they play their part.
Each moment blends, a timeless dance,
In light and dark, we find our chance.

The Illusive Embrace

In twilight's grasp, we seek to hold,
The warmth of love, a tale retold.
Yet shadows linger, a fickle friend,
In this embrace, what's real, what's pretend?

Whispers echo in a silent night,
Yearning hearts chase elusive light.
Tender glances weave a bind,
But in the distance, love's undefined.

Holding tight, yet slipping through,
Like grains of sand, we misconstrue.
Fleeting moments blur the lines,
In sweetness, bitterness entwines.

What do we gain when love can't stay?
The illusive touch, it slips away.
Still, we dance in this bittersweet space,
Finding truth in the fading embrace.

Serenity's War with Tumult

In quiet moments, peace is sought,
Yet chaos stirs, a raging thought.
Serenity dances, but stumbles too,
In the heart's battle, what's real, what's true.

Waves crash fiercely against the shore,
Echoes of calm, yet longing for more.
Stillness whispers of lost delight,
As tumult roars through the midnight.

A gentle breeze can soothe the strife,
While discord claws at the edge of life.
In shadows cast, serenity wanes,
Fighting the war that ever remains.

Yet, amidst the storm, a light will sway,
Hope flickers softly, finding a way.
In serenity's arms, we learn to survive,
Though tumult may strike, we still can thrive.

The Unruly Comfort of Ambiguity

In the space between right and wrong,
Lies a melody, a comforting song.
Ambiguity wraps its arms around,
A paradox found in confusion's sound.

A haze of gray in a world so clear,
Freedom whispers, void of fear.
Each choice a dance on a fragile thread,
In uncertainty's warmth, many fear to tread.

Yet beauty lingers in the unknown,
In realms uncharted, seeds are sown.
For in the fog of choices untold,
Lies wisdom sought by the brave and bold.

The unruly comfort sparks a fire,
To chase the elusive, to dream and aspire.
In life's vast tapestry, threads intertwine,
Ambiguity blooms, its fragrance divine.

Veils of Ambivalence

Behind the curtains of heart's desire,
Lies ambivalence, a silent fire.
In the shadows, emotions clash,
Love intertwined with a fleeting flash.

Conflicted thoughts swirl like a storm,
Each longing whisper reshaping form.
To choose is a weight, burdens ignite,
Yet ambivalence dances, a mesmerizing sight.

In moments sweet, choices decay,
Truth and doubt, in their playful ballet.
A heart that wavers finds beauty rare,
In the veils of ambivalence, we learn to care.

Yet clarity shines in the midst of strife,
A spark of resolve to awaken life.
From the tangled paths, we carve our way,
Through veils of ambivalence, bright is the day.

Shadows of Uncertainty

In whispered echoes of silent night,
Shadows lengthen, cloaked from the light.
Uncertainty lingers, a haunting trace,
Dancing like phantoms, elusive in space.

Paths unseen lay before our feet,
Questions unanswered, a bittersweet beat.
In every corner, doubt takes its hold,
Casting gray veils where dreams were bold.

Yet shadows teach in their fleeting way,
To seek the dawn in the break of day.
For in uncertainty, courage blooms,
A flower resilient, shedding its gloom.

Embrace the unknown, the journey unfolds,
A tapestry woven with stories untold.
In shadows of uncertainty, hope will spark,
Guiding our souls through the encompassing dark.

Surrendering to the Unknown

In the shadows where silence dwells,
Whispers of courage softly swell.
Each breath a leap into haze,
Trusting the path that fate displays.

Stars above, they softly gleam,
Direction found within the dream.
Letting go, I feel it rise,
Surrendering, I claim the skies.

The Labyrinth of Choices

Winding paths in twilight's glow,
Footsteps echo, fast and slow.
Every turn, a story spun,
Dreams collide, and shadows run.

Questions linger in the air,
Choices weigh beyond compare.
With each step, a chance to learn,
In this maze, for hope I yearn.

Each Step of Reflection

Pause to breathe, let moments speak,
In the stillness, wisdom peaks.
Each step unfolds the hidden truth,
Like petals of an aged youth.

Echoes of the past arise,
Guiding paths with gentle ties.
In the mirror of the heart,
Every journey plays its part.

The Space of Uncertainty

In the void where dreams may falter,
Existence asks us to alter.
Between the lines of what is known,
Lies the seed of strength unshown.

A canvas blank, potential vast,
Future woven, present cast.
Through the doubt, we find our light,
In the dark, we embrace the fight.

Beneath the Fabric of Day and Night

Beneath the fabric spun so tight,
Whispers linger in twilight's flight.
Stars awaken with silver gleam,
As shadows dance in a silent dream.

The sun bows low, the moon takes stage,
Nature turns a timeless page.
Colors blend in a gentle sigh,
Life awakens as night draws nigh.

In tender moments, time will bend,
Each breath a thread that weaves and mends.
Dreams and hopes in silence grow,
Beneath the tapestry of light's soft glow.

With every heartbeat, worlds collide,
In the secrets where we confide.
A silent promise in the night,
Binding hearts in shared delight.

Echoes of Serenity and Chaos

In the stillness, whispers call,
Softly rising, or destined to fall.
Chaos erupts in a distant roar,
Yet peace lingers on a tranquil shore.

Ripples of laughter, shadows of fear,
The melody of truth we choose to hear.
Stars above, in colors bright,
Guide the wanderers through the night.

A heartbeat quickens, the storm draws near,
Yet in the eye, there's nothing to fear.
Fragments of silence amidst the din,
Revealing the calm that lies within.

In every struggle, an echo of grace,
A dance of shadows through time and space.
Though chaos reigns, serenity fights,
In hidden corners, peace ignites.

The Spectrum of a Fleeting Thought

A moment captured, drifting fast,
Colors blending, shadows cast.
In the silence, ideas play,
Fleeting thoughts that slip away.

Each hue a memory, bright or dim,
Floating gently on a whim.
The mind's embrace, both wide and small,
A spectrum echoed within us all.

Fragments scatter, an abstract art,
Emotions painted on the heart.
In the blink of an eye, they fade,
Yet in their wake, a truth is laid.

Grasping hints of what we know,
Like a river's path, it ebbs and flows.
The beauty lies in moments caught,
In the spectrum of a fleeting thought.

In the Space Between Certainty and Doubt

In the space between what we see,
Lies a truth that sets us free.
Certainty shines like morning dew,
While shadows whisper what isn't true.

A step in faith, a leap of trust,
Navigating the void, we must.
Questions linger in the air,
Yet hope remains, a guiding flare.

Each choice we make, a bridge we build,
In the silence, the heart is filled.
Doubt can linger, heavy and sore,
But courage opens a hidden door.

Between the lines of wrong and right,
Shadows dance in the fading light.
In this balance, life is found,
A symphony of thoughts unbound.

Fractured Reflections

Mirrors crack in dim-lit rooms,
Echoes whisper through the gloom.
Shattered images dance with fright,
Lost in shadows, seeking light.

Shards of truth in silver pools,
Broken hearts, but still we choose.
Fragments glimmer, hope's appeal,
Wounds will heal, the scars conceal.

Glimpses of a life once whole,
Time a thief, it takes its toll.
Yet within the pieces lies,
A story waiting to arise.

Fractured paths that intertwine,
We grasp at dreams, a fragile line.
In every crack, a chance to see,
The beauty in our history.

Dreams in a Dappled Sky

Clouds drift softly, whispering dreams,
Sunlight dances in golden beams.
A tapestry woven in hues,
Where every heart finds its muse.

Fields of green stretch far and wide,
Beneath a heaven, vast and bright.
Colors blend, a painter's stroke,
In every hue, sweet words are spoke.

Shadows play on warm embrace,
Nature's breath, a gentle pace.
With every sigh, the world stands still,
In dappled light, we find our will.

Through the sky, our wishes soar,
Chasing horizons, forevermore.
In this realm of endless height,
We dance through day, we dream at night.

The Veil of Choices

A curtain drawn, the paths unfold,
Every choice, a story told.
Winds of fate whisper and sway,
Guiding hearts along the way.

Stepping forth with hope in hand,
Each decision, a soft command.
Trembling moments, what to take?
A leap of faith, the bonds we break.

Yet shadows loom as bright unfolds,
Every step, a truth beholds.
Weave the dreams, both bold and shy,
A tapestry against the sky.

In every choice, a lesson learned,
In every heart, a fire burned.
Together we find our way to cope,
Through the veil, we chase our hope.

Fleeting Clarity

In quiet moments, wisdom flows,
Ephemeral truths like petals close.
Transient glances, fleeting time,
A heartbeat's whisper, a gentle rhyme.

Life's illusions, like morning dew,
Glinting softly in vibrant hue.
When shadows play, the light can fade,
Yet clarity's spark can't be swayed.

Epiphanies dance on the breeze,
Moments ignite like autumn leaves.
As laughter fades into the night,
Fleeting clarity, a guiding light.

Cherish each glimpse, hold it tight,
For clarity's gift is pure delight.
In the ebb and flow, we find our way,
With every dawn, a brand new day.

Hues of Confusion

Shadows dance in twilight's glow,
Colors swirl, a vibrant flow.
Questions linger, answers fade,
In this maze, I'm disarrayed.

Brushstrokes clash with muted shades,
A canvas bright, yet truth evades.
Every hue, a tale untold,
In my heart, a storm unfolds.

Amidst the blurs, I search for grace,
Fractured pieces, a jumbled space.
Each stroke whispers, sings aloud,
In confusion, I'm proud and cowed.

Yet beauty grows in tangled thread,
As chaos reigns, my spirit's fed.
Through vibrant strife, I find my way,
In hues of night, I greet the day.

Echoes of the Apart

Voices tremble on the breeze,
Fleeting whispers, lost with ease.
In the distance, shadows call,
A haunting touch, a soul's downfall.

Memories linger, frail and thin,
Tales of love and dreams within.
Spaces widen, time decays,
Holding tightly, as hope frays.

Each echo bounces off the walls,
Fading softly as silence falls.
Fragments scatter, clear and bright,
In this void, I chase the light.

Yet in the stillness, truth reveals,
Resilience blooms, the heart now heals.
From the apart, I'll rise anew,
With echoes strong, I'll make it through.

Torn Between Two Worlds

Footsteps echo on the line,
Two paths drawn, neither mine.
Choices whisper, pull and sway,
In two worlds, I long to stay.

Familiar faces fade from sight,
While new horizons bring delight.
Dreams held close, yet drifting far,
In this tug, I bear the scar.

Moments clash, collide, and weave,
Caught in longing, never leave.
Each heartbeat feels like a sigh,
In this split, I learn to fly.

Yet harmony can find its grace,
Bridging gaps in time and space.
With open heart, I'll learn to blend,
Two worlds met, both will amend.

The Gray Horizon

A muted sky where dreams reside,
Clouds hang heavy, hearts collide.
Between the dark and light I stand,
On this gray, uncertain land.

Whispers echo through the mist,
A void of warmth, a fleeting twist.
Hope flickers in shadows' seams,
As I grasp for fading dreams.

Yet in the gray, I find my muse,
Colors blend, no time to lose.
Each shade, a lesson soft and wise,
In the depths, a spark will rise.

Though the horizon dims my view,
With every breath, I push on through.
For in the gray, I hold the key,
A world reborn, and I am free.

Shattered Rainbows in Monochrome

Once vibrant hues now fade away,
Dreams lost in a dusky gray.
Fragments drift on the cold ground,
Whispers of colors no longer found.

Every promise painted bright,
Now dissolves in the pale light.
Echoes of laughter, just a sound,
In this monochrome world, we're bound.

Memories flutter like leaves in fall,
Crushed beneath a silence's call.
Rainbows shattered, hopes entwined,
In black and white, we've been defined.

Yet in the shadows, a hint of shade,
A spark of color, gently replayed.
From fragments, we can still create,
A canvas anew, let love awake.

When Stars Hide Behind the Clouds

In the velvet night, darkness falls,
Yet a hush stirs within the walls.
Stars whisper secrets to the night,
But clouds cocoon their distant light.

Every twinkle, a story untold,
Beliefs in wishes, brave and bold.
Yet veils of gray, they drift and sway,
Hiding dreams that wander astray.

Hope lingers where shadows creep,
Beneath the clouds, mysteries sleep.
For even when stars seem afar,
Faith ignites to light the dark.

As storms brew with a turbulent roar,
We yearn for the shine we adore.
In patience, we'll find the way to see,
The stars that are hidden, still gleam for me.

The Softness of a Hard Truth

Like feathers falling, soft and light,
A truth emerges from the night.
It bears the weight of heavy tales,
Yet gently whispers as it exhales.

Hearts may tremble at what they learn,
But in acceptance, we softly yearn.
The echoes of truth can sting and bite,
Yet they cradle us with pure insight.

In honesty, we find our grace,
A moment's pause, a tender space.
Though hard to face, it carries peace,
In its embrace, all doubts may cease.

With every truth, a healing flow,
Softening scars we long to know.
In the light of what is truly right,
We find our courage, shining bright.

Chasing Shadows of the Unfamiliar

In twilight's glow, silhouettes dance,
Chasing shadows, we take a chance.
The unknown whispers in the breeze,
Urging hearts to find their ease.

Paths unworn beckon us near,
With every step, we conquer fear.
Fears may haunt like ghosts in flight,
Yet courage springs from the night.

In shadows deep, secrets reside,
We tread lightly, hearts open wide.
Venturing forth into the gray,
Each new shadow leads the way.

For in the strange, we find our song,
A melody where we belong.
In chasing shadows, we come to see,
The beauty in what's meant to be.

Layers of Deception

Beneath the smiles, a secret lies,
Wrapped in whispers, truth defies.
Veils of facades, they softly sway,
In shadows where the lost words play.

Each layer peeled reveals the dread,
Of hidden paths that we have tread.
Masking sorrow with a grin,
The dance of lies will soon begin.

Echoes linger, haunting the night,
When honesty flees, and darkness bites.
A shroud of dreams, we choose to wear,
In crumbled hopes and silent despair.

Yet in the depths, a spark remains,
A chance to break the stifling chains.
To cast aside the weight we bear,
And find the truth that lingers there.

The Jigsaw of Being

Life's a puzzle, pieces scattered,
We search for edges, questions shattered.
In every turn, a story spun,
A fleeting moment, life is begun.

Colors blend, and shadows fight,
Fragments whisper in the night.
We fit together, piece by piece,
Seeking solace, a sweet release.

Each loss and gain shapes who we are,
In this great maze, we wander far.
Threading memories, hopes entwined,
A jigsaw heart, by fate defined.

Yet even in chaos, beauty shows,
In mismatched corners, love still grows.
Every crack, a lesson learned,
In the jigsaw of being, we are turned.

Misty Truths

In morning's haze, the world awakes,
With veils of grey, the daylight breaks.
Hidden whispers in the fog,
Mysteries linger like a dog.

Shadows dance on silent trees,
As secrets murmur with the breeze.
Things unseen, yet felt so deep,
In the stillness, thoughts will seep.

Truths lie cloaked in shades of mist,
A gentle beckon, an urge to twist.
Finding clarity through the shroud,
In soft embraces, unseen, loud.

Yet when the sun breaks through the gloom,
Revealing goodness, dispelling doom.
In clarity, our hearts align,
Embracing truths, the heart does shine.

A Balancing Act

Life's tightrope stretches, thin and high,
With every step, we reach for the sky.
Between joy and sorrow, we tread the line,
A balancing act that's truly divine.

Dreams and fears, they dance around,
In the silence, they make a sound.
With courage found in the midst of doubt,
We learn to walk, to live, to shout.

Each stumble teaches, each fall prepares,
For the grace we find when life ensnares.
With open arms, we gather strength,
In this act of life, we find our length.

So take a breath, embrace the ride,
In every challenge, let love abide.
For in this dance, we learn our way,
A balancing act, come what may.

Shades of Irresolution

In shadows dance the thoughts we chase,
Flickering doubts across our face.
Each step forward, a lingering fight,
Caught in the web of day and night.

Choices whisper in a muted tone,
A heart divided, forever alone.
Paths diverge like branches in trees,
Guiding us softly, with half-hearted pleas.

The clock ticks on with muted calls,
Echoing softly as resolve falls.
In the maze of maybe, we remain,
Forever trapped within our own refrain.

Yet here we stand, on edges drawn,
Wishing for clarity with the dawn.
Though lost in shades of uncertain light,
We'll seek our truth beyond the night.

The Silence of Sorrows

In the corners where shadows creep,
Lies a silence far too deep.
Whispers of pain hold the air,
Emotions sealed, fragile and rare.

Memories linger like ghosts on walls,
Echoing soft, as the heart calls.
Each tear unshed, a mournful song,
Carried in hearts where they belong.

Time may fade the sharpest edge,
Yet sorrow lingers as a pledge.
In quiet moments, it leaves its mark,
A gentle ache deep in the dark.

But within the silence, strength will rise,
A beacon shining in the skies.
For every sorrow, a lesson learned,
In the stillness, a fire burned.

Navigating the Numb

In the fog where feelings blur,
Waves of silence softly stir.
Drifting through the hazy dread,
Chasing shadows of what's said.

Beneath the surface, echoes lie,
Unseen currents, hard to defy.
We search for warmth in frozen nights,
Longing for the wish of lights.

Every heartbeat seems subdued,
Emotions tucked away, unviewed.
Heavy eyes in a world so vast,
Yearning for a moment to last.

Yet in the stillness, hope will bloom,
From cracks in the cold, the heart finds room.
Navigating through this quiet sea,
One day we'll awaken, truly free.

Starlight in the Gloom

Amidst the dark where shadows play,
Stars whisper secrets of the day.
Beneath the weight of weary skies,
Hope flickers softly, never dies.

In the stillness, dreams take flight,
Guided by the distant light.
Through the gloom, we weave our way,
Hand in hand, come what may.

Though storms may rage, and winds may sway,
Our spirits rise with each new ray.
For in the depths, the star remains,
A shining spark through all the pains.

So here we stand, against the stream,
Holding tight to every dream.
In every shadow, find the gleam,
Starlight shines bright, a radiant beam.

A Symphony of Contrasting Whispers

In twilight's glow, shadows dance,
Whispers collide in sweet romance.
Silent echoes pierce the night,
Harmony found in dissonant light.

Branches sway with tender grace,
While storms approach, quicken the pace.
Each note a secret, softly played,
In the silence, worries fade.

Colors clash in vivid dreams,
Life unfolds in fervent schemes.
Yet within the chaos lies,
The beauty where each contrast ties.

In every heart, a song resides,
A symphony where fate abides.
Through the storms and gentle graces,
We find ourselves in hidden places.

The Illusion of Stillness in Motion

Ripples stretch across the lake,
Stillness holds, but hearts awake.
Leaves may float, yet winds will guide,
In this calm, the truths abide.

The world spins on without rest,
Moments blend, we feel them best.
Like shadows morphing in the skies,
Change occurs while stillness lies.

Time cascades like falling leaves,
In its grasp, our spirit weaves.
What seems still, is ever free,
In the motion, we find glee.

In the quiet, listen close,
The heartbeats hum, we feel the prose.
With each breath, the world will sway,
An illusion, in bright display.

Colors That Fade in Unison

Sunset hues in soft decay,
Gold and crimson drift away.
Fading into night's embrace,
Life's kaleidoscope, a chase.

Brushstrokes blend on canvas bare,
Memories caught in muted air.
Each shade whispers tales untold,
In silence, a legacy bold.

Flowers wilt in the autumn breeze,
Petals crumble from the trees.
Yet in the loss, a beauty lies,
Nature cycles, never dies.

Colors shift beneath the sun,
Every ending's just begun.
In fading light, we learn to see,
Life's rich tapestry, wild and free.

Beneath the Surface of Serene Waters

Below the calm, a world concealed,
Mysteries of silence revealed.
Fish darting in fluid grace,
Time suspended in this place.

Reflections shimmer, soft and bright,
Echoing dreams in the soft twilight.
Gentle currents tell their tales,
In whispered forms, where time prevails.

Bubbles rise like fleeting thoughts,
Within the depths, calmness caught.
Nature breathes a tranquil sigh,
As ripples dance and shadows lie.

In serene waters, we will dive,
Finding peace as we revive.
Beneath the surface, secrets grow,
A silent world with much to show.

Navigating the Unclear Path

Through the fog, I stumble slow,
Whispers guide where I should go.
Stars hidden in the shrouded night,
Footsteps falter, seeking light.

Twisting routes, a maze of doubt,
Every choice feels like a rout.
Yet I tread, with heart held high,
Determined still, I will not die.

In the stillness, clarity calls,
As shadows dance on crumbling walls.
I breathe deep, let my fears release,
Finding strength in the search for peace.

With each step, the path unfolds,
A story written, dreams retold.
Though uncertain, I will prevail,
Navigating this winding trail.

Half-Lit Realizations

In the dusk, I catch a glimpse,
Thoughts like shadows, dance and limp.
Half-lit truths, both warm and cold,
Secrets whispered, yet untold.

Moments linger, then they fade,
Memories in twilight made.
Bright illusions start to break,
Sifting through the noise, awake.

Awareness glimmers through the haze,
In fleeting thoughts, my spirit sways.
A heart once heavy starts to soar,
As half-lit dreams unlock the door.

Within this space, I start to find,
A richer world, both bold and blind.
Through soft focus, I will see,
The beauty in this mystery.

The Weight of Tomorrow

In the silence, burdens grow,
Futures whispered, winds bestow.
Each decision, heavy chains,
As my heart feels all the strains.

Tomorrow's hopes, a double edge,
Promises made, I now pledge.
Yet the fear of what may come,
Makes my spirit feel so numb.

Yet I hold this weight with grace,
Each heartbeat, a steady pace.
Underneath the load, I thrive,
Finding strength to still revive.

With each dawn, I rise anew,
Casting off what once I knew.
The weight shall not define my way,
I choose to face a brighter day.

Eclipsed Expectations

In shadows cast by what should be,
I wander through my reverie.
Expectations like the sun,
Outshone by what I've become.

In silence, dreams begin to change,
Life unfolds in ways so strange.
What I thought would lead to light,
Turns to dusk, veiled from sight.

Yet in this dark, I find my fire,
Passion blooms, hearts never tire.
Eclipsed, but not erased away,
I forge my path, come what may.

In the stillness, possibility sings,
A world reborn, on new wings.
Through eclipsed expectations, I see,
Life's true wonders set me free.

The Fraying Threads

In shadows where the fabric fades,
The delicate weave begins to fray.
Each whisper carries secrets made,
Lost echoes of the light of day.

A tapestry of dreams, half spun,
Threads of gold and silver gleam.
Yet in the dark, they come undone,
A fleeting touch, a vanishing dream.

The hands that wove, now ghostly pale,
Count the stitches, one by one.
A story told within the frail,
Yet yearning hearts, they come undone.

In fragile seams, our hopes remain,
A patchwork of both joy and sorrow.
Though time may weave with strength and strain,
The fraying threads hold life's tomorrow.

Lurking in the Twilight

The moonlight dances on the ground,
As shadows stretch and softly sigh.
In the dusk, secrets abound,
Whispers linger, fading shy.

Figures lurking, shades of night,
In the corners of our dreams.
A world that hides from morning light,
Where reality's not what it seems.

The trees sway gently, secrets weave,
Branches curling in the hush.
In this realm, we dare believe,
That dreams awaken with a rush.

As daylight fades, we come alive,
In twilight's arms, we find our way.
With every breath, our souls survive,
A lingered hope, the night will stay.

Embracing the Ambiguous

In the shades of gray, we wander lost,
Between the lines that twist and turn.
What really matters? What's the cost?
In every question, we discern.

The beauty lies in what's unclear,
Where paths diverge and merge again.
With open hearts, we face our fear,
As life's great puzzles bring us pain.

Not every answer brings us peace,
In doubts, we cultivate our trust.
From uncertainty, we find release,
In chaos, we build bridges of dust.

In every moment, let us pause,
To cherish life's uncertain dance.
In ambiguity, we find cause,
To hold on tight and take a chance.

Color in the Chaos

In the storm, a splash of hue,
Paint the world with every tear.
Amidst the noise, the heart stays true,
Bringing focus, bringing cheer.

With every brushstroke, light ignites,
A canvas full of twisted shade.
In the wild, we chase the sights,
In chaos, beauty is laid.

From every clash, a story blooms,
Vivid shades in shadows play.
In life's great noise, hear love's tunes,
Color brightens up the gray.

So let the chaos swirl and spin,
For in the chaos, we shall thrive.
With vibrant dreams, we'll dance and grin,
Finding color, feeling alive.

Whispers of Dusk and Dawn

The sun dips low, a mellow glow,
Whispers soft, where shadows flow.
Cool winds carry secrets spun,
As night embraces day's soft run.

Stars awaken, their twinkling eyes,
In the quiet, the world sighs.
Dreams take flight on gentle breeze,
In twilight, all the heart's at ease.

The horizon glows, a painted hue,
As darkness wraps the world anew.
Hope slips softly into night,
While dawn will bring the morning light.

In whispers of dusk, we find our way,
Through shadows deep, till break of day.
Each moment holds a chance to find,
The beauty woven in mankind.

Shadows That Dance in Dilemmas

In corners dark, shadows creep,
Whispers of choices that run deep.
Every decision, a haunting face,
In the dance of time, we find our place.

Flickering lights cast doubts so bold,
In the grip of fear, hearts grow cold.
Yet within the trials we endure,
Are lessons learned, a soul made sure.

Mirrored reflections twist and sway,
Showing the paths we choose each day.
Lost in the maze of what we seek,
In shadows that dance, we're made unique.

Each dilemma close, a silent plea,
To understand who we're meant to be.
As shadows whirl in the hazy light,
We brave the darkness, embrace the fight.

The Veil of Truth and Illusion

A silver veil drapes to conceal,
In whispers soft, our fates reveal.
Truth may shimmer, at times deceive,
While shadows linger, we believe.

Through twists of fate, we wander wide,
In the dawn of dreams where hopes collide.
Illusions dance, a splendid game,
Yet truth remains, though hard to claim.

Beneath the surface, layers hide,
A tender heart, a shrouded pride.
With every choice, we seek to find,
The essence pure that lies behind.

In the lace of night, we search for light,
In understanding, we'll find what's right.
To lift the veil, and dare to see,
The depth of truth that sets us free.

Duality in Silken Skies

Beneath the heavens, a silent grace,
Day and night in a warm embrace.
Clouds like dreams drift quick and slow,
In colors bright, a vibrant show.

Stars align in a cosmic weave,
One heart breaks, another believes.
In shadows deep, in light so bright,
The dance of duality takes its flight.

Every heartbeat, a contradiction,
In peace and chaos, our conviction.
A gaze above, where worlds collide,
In silken skies, we glide and hide.

Embrace the night, rejoice the morn,
In every ending, a new hope born.
Explore the depths of both the high,
For life's a canvas, painted sky.

Threads of the Unknown

In the shadows where secrets weave,
Whispers of fate begin to conceive,
A tapestry of dreams untold,
Woven in silence, both timid and bold.

Through hidden paths where mysteries lie,
Shimmering strands in the ink-dark sky,
Each flicker a story, a chance to unfold,
Threads of the unknown, both fiery and cold.

With curious hands, we seek the light,
Unraveling knots that bind day and night,
In every twist, a choice to make,
The fabric of life, a fragile awake.

So tread with care on this delicate seam,
For in the unknown, we find our dream,
And in the weaving, our spirits rise,
Threads of the unknown, a path to the skies.

The Balmy Breeze

The balmy breeze whispers soft and low,
Carrying secrets from places we know,
It dances on leaves, a gentle caress,
Bringing us peace, a moment to bless.

In twilight's glow, it weaves through the trees,
Swaying the branches with effortless ease,
A touch of the ocean, a hint of the sun,
The balmy breeze whispers, inviting us to run.

It travels through fields, over valleys so wide,
Kisses the flowers where dreams abide,
A song of the earth, a sweet, tender tune,
The balmy breeze hums to the light of the moon.

So let us embrace this airy embrace,
And dance with the wind in this sacred place,
For in every sigh, it brings us alive,
The balmy breeze is where we thrive.

Veils of the Mind

Behind the veils where thoughts intertwine,
Shadows flicker, bright yet malign,
A labyrinth spun from the threads of our fears,
Memories echo, and laughter appears.

In chambers of silence, our whispers reside,
Buried emotions we seek and hide,
Each layer we peel, a truth to explore,
Veils of the mind holding mysteries galore.

With courage, we venture, our hearts now unchained,
Facing the darkness where ghosts have remained,
For every revealing, a chance to be free,
Veils of the mind, let the light finally see.

So dare to uncover, don't shy from the pain,
Embrace every tear, each joy, every stain,
For beneath the surface, we grow and we find,
The beauty in peeling the veils of the mind.

Sunlight Through the Gloom

When shadows gather, thick like a cloak,
And whispers of doubt in the stillness provoke,
A sliver of hope breaks through the night,
Sunlight pours in, igniting the fight.

In moments of darkness, we search for the spark,
Light dances our fears, dispels the stark,
With every beam, our spirits soar high,
Sunlight through gloom, a tender reply.

Each ray a promise, a warm, guiding hand,
Leading us forth to a brighter land,
In the heart of despair, there's a flicker, a glow,
Sunlight through gloom, a path we can follow.

So hold to the light, let it fill every room,
For life's sweetest music can bloom from the gloom,
Where darkness once lingered, now shines the day,
Sunlight through gloom leads the weary away.

Emblazoned Contradictions

In shadows bright and colors stark,
Love wears the mask of bitter dark.
Hope flickers low in raging flames,
Yet dances still in whispered games.

A vibrant truth wrapped up in lies,
A joyous heart that softly sighs.
The thorns that prick, the roses sweet,
Forge beauty found in tangled feet.

With every step, a conflict's call,
A rise, a fall, a rise, a fall.
We paint our dreams with fractured hues,
In contradicted paths we choose.

So let us wade through vibrant strife,
Embracing contrasts, loving life.
For in the clash, we find our way,
A vibrant dawn breaks into day.

Forming Fables in the Mist

Through veils of fog, stories evolve,
Where ancient whispers start to solve.
The moonlight drips on silken threads,
As dreams awaken from their beds.

Each tale unfolds with hidden pasts,
In shadows where the wisdom lasts.
Characters born from whispered lore,
In every heart, they yearn for more.

A secret path, a twist of fate,
Where folklore breathes and hearts await.
In murmurs soft, the legends call,
With every breath, a fable's thrall.

So wander forth through misty air,
Embrace the stories everywhere.
For in this haze, the truth remains,
A tapestry of joys and pains.

Undefined Horizons

On edges blurred, where shadows lie,
The sun dips low, a whispered sigh.
Dreams stretch out, like fingers wide,
Reaching for what's undefined.

Margins melt where colors blend,
Tomorrow's hope, today we send.
A restless heart, a yearning gaze,
Exploring paths through sunlit haze.

The sky unfurls in shades unknown,
Each step beyond, a seed is sown.
In every breath, new worlds appear,
To chase the light, to shed the fear.

So rise with dawn, embrace the quest,
To seek the place where dreams can rest.
Undefined, yet ever bright,
Horizons call, a guiding light.

The Churn of Doubt

Within the mind, a storm does brew,
As shadows dance, the questions grew.
A tempest tosses thoughts around,
In churns of doubt, we're often bound.

A whispered fear, a lingering strife,
The push and pull, the weight of life.
We search for truth within the haze,
Yet clarity slips through the maze.

In moments dim, the heart retreats,
To quiet corners, hidden beats.
But in the chaos, strength is found,
In searching depths, our roots are bound.

So face the tides, embrace the fray,
Let doubt dissolve, come what may.
For in the churn, we glimpse the grace,
That guides us through this wondrous space.

Dreams Woven from Twilight's Embrace

In the hush of evening's glow,
Dreams begin to softly flow.
Threads of gold and silver light,
Knit together through the night.

Whispers dance on gentle air,
Secrets linger everywhere.
Stars awaken, shy and bright,
Guiding souls in tranquil flight.

Time stands still, a heartbeat's pause,
Nature's beauty earns applause.
Woven tales of joy and pain,
Bring the heart to love again.

As the dawn approaches near,
Twilight's magic disappears.
Yet the dreams, though dimmed, remain,
Carried forth through joy and strain.

The Light that Lingers in the Gloom

When shadows stretch and fears abound,
A flicker of hope can be found.
In the corners, soft and warm,
A gentle light begins to form.

It dances on the edges, free,
A beacon for the lost to see.
When darkness tries to claim the day,
This light will guide, will lead the way.

Though storms may rage and tempests howl,
The heart finds strength, begins to growl.
For in the gloom, we learn to fight,
With courage borne from inner light.

In every tear, in every sigh,
The light will lift us, by and by.
Within the gloom, we find our spark,
Illuminating paths through the dark.

Misty Echoes of Silent Strife

In the fog that cloaks the morn,
Silent battles rage, forlorn.
Voices lost in whispers spread,
Echoes of the words unsaid.

Hearts are heavy, shadows creep,
In the silence, secrets sleep.
Yet beneath the mist, a flame,
Flickers softly to sustain.

Every struggle, every tear,
Shapes the soul, erases fear.
With every echo, we will rise,
Finding strength in our goodbyes.

Through the mist, a path will clear,
Guided by the light we steer.
Misty echoes, deep and rife,
Lead us to a fuller life.

Fractured Reflections in a Crystal Sky

Beneath the vast, unyielding blue,
Fractured dreams come into view.
Shattered pieces, lost in flight,
Twinkling stars embrace the night.

Each reflection tells a tale,
Of victories and love so frail.
Mirrored hopes in silent cry,
Glimmer softly, never die.

The crystal sky, a canvas wide,
Holds the laughter, holds the pride.
In every shard, a story lives,
Broken hearts yet still forgive.

As dawn breaks through the night's refrain,
Fragments dance like gentle rain.
In every fracture, beauty lies,
Found in fractured, crystal skies.

The Weight of Lightness

In shadows deep, the light does play,
A feather's touch, a whisper's sway.
It lifts the heart, yet holds it tight,
A paradox in day and night.

The smiles we wear, the laughter shared,
Yet burdens hide, no one is spared.
Each joyful glance, a fleeting fight,
The weight of lightness feels so right.

We dance on air, but roots are deep,
In silence, secrets softly creep.
The brighter days, the darkened nights,
A balance born of gentle flights.

So let us cherish every spark,
The calm of day, the peace of dark.
For in this world of joy and strife,
We find the beauty, through this life.

A Dance of Sorrow and Joy

In twilight's glow, the shadows wane,
A tender heart bears hidden pain.
Yet in the sorrow, joy will bloom,
A dance entwined within the gloom.

With every step, the heart will sway,
Through bitter nights and brighter days.
A symphony of grief and cheer,
In life's grand waltz, we persevere.

Each tear that falls, a lesson learned,
In flame of joy, our spirits burned.
We twirl in circles, lost in time,
A rhythm found in every rhyme.

So hold me close, through thick and thin,
In every loss, a chance to win.
For sorrow's song and joy's sweet play,
Together weave our endless way.

The Unseen Threads of Fate's Weaving

In quiet corners, threads entwine,
A tapestry of fate divine.
With every stitch, a story spun,
A whispered truth, the threads are one.

Across the loom, the colors blend,
Where destiny and choice descend.
Each knot a moment, woven tight,
In shadowed hours and morning light.

We pull the strings, yet feel their pull,
A dance of chance, a heart so full.
Unseen connections, paths unseen,
In life's great weave, we find the sheen.

So trust the yarn that guides your hands,
Through tangled paths, our spirit stands.
For in this weave of fate and dreams,
We find our strength in quiet seams.

Between the Lines of Laughter and Tears

In laughter's echo, joy takes flight,
Yet tears can dance in the same light.
A fragile line, so thinly drawn,
Between the dusk and the bright dawn.

With every smile, a shadow lurks,
In playful jest, a truth that works.
The heart will ache, then rise anew,
In every laugh, a tear slips through.

The stories bind us, joy and pain,
In every loss, there's much to gain.
Between the lines, we find our way,
In laughter's grip, in sorrow's sway.

So let us cherish every phase,
In every tear, a love that stays.
Between the lines, we weave our tale,
In laughter's song, we shall prevail.

Whispers in the Fog

In the stillness of dawn's embrace,
Soft whispers curl and trace.
Shadows dance where secrets lie,
Veiled in the mist, they sigh.

Footsteps lost in emerald dreams,
Nature's hush, all is as it seems.
Delicate echoes weave the air,
A world enchanted, beyond compare.

Through the shroud where spirits glide,
Voices gently ebb and slide.
Magic lingers in the gray,
Carrying thoughts of yesterday.

As the sun begins to rise,
Fog retreats, a sweet goodbye.
Yet in memory, it stays aglow,
Those whispers soft, forever flow.

Tangled in Duality

In shadows cast by flickering light,
Two paths merge, an endless fight.
A dance of dark and of the bright,
Life's canvas painted with insight.

Joy entwined with threads of pain,
Sunshine kissed by soft, warm rain.
In every loss, there lies a gain,
A gentle balance we can't feign.

Reflections swirl in calm and storm,
A heart that bends yet stays warm.
Unity found in the divide,
Embracing what we cannot hide.

Thus we wander, hand in hand,
Through contradictions we understand.
In duality's embrace, we grow,
Two sides of the same cherished glow.

Light Beneath the Mist

Beneath the veil of silver sheen,
Glows a light, soft and serene.
Hidden gems in nature's fold,
Stories of the brave and bold.

Layers whisper, secrets deep,
In the hush, the world does sleep.
A flicker shines, a call to see,
Hope ignites like a wild free.

Mist cascading, dreams take flight,
Guiding souls through silent night.
Warmth emerges, shadows flee,
A dance of light, wild and free.

Each heartbeat thrums, a pulse of grace,
Life awakens in this space.
Underneath the muted shroud,
We find strength, fierce and proud.

Paradox of the Sky

In twilight's glow, the sun does sink,
While stars arise, they brightly wink.
An endless loop, day meets night,
In paradox, we find our light.

Clouds can weep, yet bring forth rain,
From sorrow's depths, we rise again.
The sky can storm, then calm can chase,
In every shift, we find our place.

Eternal dance of dusk and dawn,
In shadows deep, new hopes are drawn.
With each horizon, truths are etched,
A mystery, forever stretched.

So let us marvel at the skies,
In every end, new journey lies.
Through paradox, our spirits soar,
In endless wonder, we explore.

The Edge of Discontent

On the brink of silent cries,
Where shadows dance and dreams disguise.
Fingers clutch at empty space,
In the mirror, an unfamiliar face.

Restlessness whispers through the night,
A flickering flame, a fading light.
Hope clings tightly, then slips away,
As night wrestles with the day.

Chains of sorrow, heavy still,
Confined within a restless will.
Beyond the edge, what lies in wait?
A garden grown from seeds of fate.

Yet in the echoes, a voice remains,
Beneath the weight of unseen chains.
Seeking solace in scattered dreams,
On the edge where nothing seems.

Glimpses of Harmony

In quiet spaces, whispers blend,
Notes of joy around the bend.
Nature hums a gentle song,
Where hearts unite and fears grow strong.

Morning rays break through the night,
Shadows fade, revealing sight.
In every smile, a story weaves,
The dance of life, as the heart believes.

Together we tread on paths adorned,
With laughter's echoes, we are reborn.
Hands reach out, a soft embrace,
In unity, we find our place.

Glimmers shine in deepest night,
Threads of hope, shimmering bright.
In each moment, harmony sings,
A tapestry of all our things.

Inverted Clarity

Beneath the surface, truths collide,
In shadows where our fears abide.
Reflections dance, a twisted view,
The world unwinds, creating new.

What is clear in this strange light,
Is often lost in the silent fight.
Questions linger, answers shy,
Inverted clarity, we wonder why.

Moments flicker, shifting fast,
Lessons learned, grasped, and passed.
Chasing visions that intertwine,
In the chaos, we seek a sign.

Yet, in the labyrinth, we will find,
The beauty held in the undefined.
Through the maze of doubt and fear,
Emerges clarity, crystal clear.

The Lure of the Unseen

In whispers soft, the unknown calls,
Through darkened woods where shadows fall.
A fleeting vision, a phantom trace,
The unseen world, an enticing embrace.

Fingers reach for what lies beyond,
The echo of a distant song.
Mysteries lurk in every breath,
A riveting dance with life and death.

What hides just out of sight,
Beckons us with soft delight.
In the silence, secrets unfold,
In tales of wonder, waiting to be told.

Drawn like moths to a hidden flame,
We crave the wild, the untamed name.
The unseen promises to astound,
In every heartbeat, the magic found.

Unraveled Threads of Thought

In the quiet of the mind, threads unwind,
Thoughts scatter like leaves in the breeze.
Each whisper echoes, a puzzle to find,
Memories linger, a playful tease.

Woven through dreams, a tapestry bright,
Fragments of stories, both bitter and sweet.
Every heartbeat carries a flickering light,
Guiding us forward, our lives to complete.

Lost in the maze of a wandering mind,
Questions arise with no clear reply.
Seeking the solace that's hard to find,
In the threads of thought, we learn to fly.

And as dusk descends like a gentle sigh,
We wrap ourselves in the warmth of the past.
Embracing the moments, as we learn to try,
Unraveled threads that forever last.

Haze of the Heart's Confusion

In the depth of silence, shadows entwine,
Whispers of longing that dance in the night.
Heartbeats collide, no reason nor rhyme,
Searching for clarity, seeking the light.

The fog stretches thick, like a lover's embrace,
Veiling the edges, where truth hides away.
Eyes wide with wonder, lost in the chase,
Navigating feelings, we sway and we sway.

Words become heavy, each syllable weighs,
A melody playing beneath veils of doubt.
In the haze, we wander through tumultuous days,
Driven by passion we cannot live without.

With every heartbeat, the confusion grows,
Yet hope flickers softly, a candle's glint.
In the haze of the heart, the warmth still flows,
Guiding us gently through shadows, we hint.

Storms Beneath a Quiet Surface

Calm waters shimmer, a deceptive guise,
Beneath, the turmoil stirs restless and wild.
In silence, a tempest brews, unseen ties,
The calm before chaos, the tension compiled.

Reflections mislead, a tranquil façade,
Yet echoes reverberate deep in the soul.
Waves crashing inward, emotion is marred,
What lies beneath takes a heavy toll.

The heart beats fiercely, like thunder's own roar,
Lightning strikes swiftly, illuminating truth.
To navigate waters, we must explore,
Embracing the chaos to free the uncouth.

For storms can refine, as much as they hurt,
Shaping the essence of who we become.
From the depths of the struggle, we unearth,
A calm that emerges, a resolute hum.

Paradox in Every Breath

Every breath a paradox, life intertwined,
In moments of laughter, we find our sorrow.
Joy and despair, a dance so aligned,
Echoing truths that we still must borrow.

The sun softly rises, yet shadows encroach,
Carrying warmth where the cold does reside.
In dreams we are fearless, yet doubt can encroach,
Navigating desires and fears side by side.

Every heartbeat pulses with joy and regret,
A tapestry woven of triumph and strife.
In the paradox seasoned, we learn to forget,
And cherish the moments that color our life.

So embrace the enigma, let it unfold,
For in every breath lies a story untold.
To dance with the paradox, fearless and bold,
Is to truly live, a journey to behold.

Milton Keynes UK
Ingram Content Group UK Ltd.
UKHW022118251124
451529UK00012B/582